YOU'RE PART OF A
STATE
COMMUNITY!

BY THERESA EMMINIZER

Gareth Stevens
PUBLISHING

Please visit our website, www.garethstevens.com. For a free color catalog of all our high-quality books, call toll free 1-800-542-2595 or fax 1-877-542-2596.

Cataloging-in-Publication Data

Names: Emminizer, Theresa.
Title: You're part of a state community! / Theresa Emminizer
Description: New York : Gareth Stevens Publishing, 2020. | Series: All our communities | Includes glossary and index.
Identifiers: ISBN 9781538245453 (pbk.) | ISBN 9781538245477 (library bound) | ISBN 9781538245460 (6 pack)
Subjects: LCSH:State governments–United States–Juvenile literature. | Community life--Juvenile literature.
Classification: LCC JK2408.E463 2020 | DDC 320.473–dc23

Published in 2020 by
Gareth Stevens Publishing
111 East 14th Street, Suite 349
New York, NY 10003

Designer: Sarah Liddell
Editor: Theresa Emminizer

Photo credits: cover, p. 1 (girl) iofoto/Shutterstock.com; cover, p. 1 (boy) Jeka/Shutterstock.com; background texture used throughout april70/Shutterstock.com; papercut texture used throughout Paladjai/Shutterstock.com; p. 5 MattiaATH/Shutterstock.com; p. 7 Pressmaster/Shutterstock.com; p. 9 Felix Lipov/Shutterstock.com; p. 11 Rob Crandall/Shutterstock.com; p. 13 wavebreakmedia/Shutterstock.com; p. 15 Box Lab/Shutterstock.com; p. 17 GABRIELLE LURIE/Stringer/AFP/Getty Images; p. 19 Dmytro Zinkevych/Shutterstock.com; p. 21 SinnartCJ/Shutterstock.com.

Printed in the United States of America

Some of the images in this book illustrate individuals who are models. The depictions do not imply actual situations or events.

CPSIA compliance information: Batch #CW20GS: For further information contact Gareth Stevens, New York, New York at 1-800-542-2595.

CONTENTS

Boldface words appear in the glossary.

Fifty States

What state do you live in? It might be in the southern United States where Texas borders Mexico, in the northern United States where Alaska borders Canada, or someplace in between! Each of America's 50 states has its own community.

Your State Community

A community is a group of people living and working together. Every person living in your state is part of your state community. That means leaders, such as people in government, and everyday people like your friends and neighbors are part of your community.

7

State Government

Each state has its own government and set of laws. The governor is the leader of the state government. State governments are in charge of taking care of the health, **education**, and **welfare** of the citizens, or people who live there.

STATE OF UTAH.

9

Citizens' Roles

State governments are made up of **representatives** who have been **elected** by the people. Citizens choose how the state will be run by voting for these leaders. Each citizen has a voice and a special role, or part to play.

Where Do You Fit?

Your state government makes decisions that **influence** your day-to-day life. As such, it's important for you to take an **active** role within your state community. Even if you aren't old enough to vote, there are many ways to take part.

Learn About Your State

Learning about your state's history can be a fun way to take an active role in your state community. When did your state become a state? What does your state **flag** look like? Does your state have a motto, or saying?

Join In

You can also be a good community member by participating, or taking part in, community **events**. You could march in a parade, gather canned goods for people in need, or raise money for a cause you feel strongly about.

Lead by Example

A positive state community starts with everyday people, just like you. By following the rules, being kind to your neighbors, and keeping your community clean, you can show others how to make your state a place to be proud of.

You and Your Community

The state you live in is a part of you and you are part of it. You have the power to make your state community a better place. People in communities, whether big or small, need to help one another. Start today!

GLOSSARY

active: participating in a group or organization's activities, or things done for a particular purpose

education: the process of teaching and learning in schools

elected: chosen for a government position

event: something that happens at a given place or time

flag: a piece of cloth with a certain pattern for a state, country, or group

influence: to have an effect on

representative: a person who stands for a group of people

welfare: well-being

FOR MORE INFORMATION

BOOKS

Machajewski, Sarah. *What Are State and Local Governments?* New York, NY: Britannica Educational Publishing, 2016.

Nagle, Jeanne. *What Is a Community?* New York, NY: Britannica Educational Publishing, 2018.

WEBSITES

Britannica Kids
kids.britannica.com/kids/article/community/626292
Learn more about what it means to be part of a community.

Du#ksters Education Site
ducksters.com/history/us_state_and_local_governments.php
Discover how state and local governments work.

INDEX